DIVINE LOVE

LENT - HOLY WEEK - EASTER

A Devotional Inspired by Nature: Volume 4

Shirley D. Andrews

WestBow Press books may be ordered through booksellers or by contacting:

WestBow Press
A Division of Thomas Nelson & Zondervan
1663 Liberty Drive
Bloomington, IN 47403
www.westbowpress.com
844-714-3454

ISBN: 978-1-6642-1274-9 (sc)
ISBN: 978-1-6642-1275-6 (e)

Library of Congress Control Number: 2020922682

Print information available on the last page.

WestBow Press rev. date: 03/01/2021

CONTENTS

ACKNOWLEDGMENTS

A special thank you to those who lifted this project to God in prayer and have continually given me words of encouragement. Your prayers and support were essential in taking this devotional from vision to reality. I am especially appreciative of:

J. Michael Fuller, a generous photographer extraordinaire and praying friend whose photography inspired my writing in each part of DIVINE LOVE, Lent – Holy Week – Easter: A Devotional Inspired by Nature: Volume 4.

Johanna Calabro, loving friend and intercessor, for her prayers, love and encouragement along this journey of faith and writing, especially her prayers.

Kendra McDonald, my loving granddaughter, who helped me design the cover for this devotional.

Cliff Fontana, a loving friend and a marketing consultant for on-line advertising and virtual reality applications.

A special thank you to those whose endorsements have blessed me and encouraged me to keep moving forward in a writing ministry for the purpose of making disciples of Jesus Christ for the transformation of the world:

The Rev. Judy Humphrey - Fox, Elder, Upper New York Annual Conference of the United Methodist Church, Pastor, Amsterdam United Methodist Church and Restoration Ministry, a bilingual New Faith Community in Amsterdam, New York.

The Rev. Brooke Newell, Elder, Upper New York Annual Conference of the United Methodist Church, Pastor, Queensbury United Methodist Church in Queensbury, New York.

PART 1

LENT

THE "KING OF LOVE" FASTS AND PRAYS IN THE DESERT

Ash Wednesday, a different date in February from year to year, is the start of a very special season of commitment for Christians to journey with Jesus Christ back to the Cross of Calvary. It is forty days of repentance with consecration and includes devotional reading, bible study, confession, repentance and intercession, a time to draw closer to God with prayer and fasting. **"Draw close to God and He will draw close to you." James 4:8.** Special worship services during the week are added for believers and to introduce unbelievers to Christ and Him crucified; and to reflect on His 40 days of fasting and prayer in the desert. There, alone, He was tempted by Satan but He remained pure and sinless by quoting the written word, the Bible, and the enemy fled. If we are living "in Christ" that victory is ours as well. We can study the word and use the word of God to protect ourselves from the deception of the enemy, Satan. He is also known as "a liar" and "the accuser of the brethren." Next is how Jesus spends time in the desert.

"Jesus, full of the Holy Spirit, returned from the Jordan River and was led by the Spirit in the desert, where for forty days he was tempted by the devil. He ate nothing during those days, and at the end of them he was hungry. The devil said to him, 'if you are the Son of God, tell this stone to become bread.' Jesus answered, 'it is written: Man does not live on bread alone.' The devil led him up to a high place and showed him in an instant all the kingdoms of the world. And he said to him, 'I will give you all their authority and splendor, for it has been given to me, and I can give it to anyone I want to. So, if you worship me, it will all be yours.' Jesus answered, 'it is written: worship the Lord your God and serve him only.'" Luke 4: 1-7 Verses 8-12 continues the dialog between Jesus and the devil. **vs.13 – "When the devil had finished all this tempting, he left Jesus until an opportune time."** From the desert Jesus returns to Galilee. He taught in the synagogues and everyone praised Him. Then He went to Nazareth where He had been brought up. He entered the synagogue there on the Sabbath as was His custom. **"The scroll of the prophet Isaiah was handed to him. He read: 'The Spirit of the Lord is on me, because he has anointed me to preach the good news to the poor. He has sent me to proclaim freedom for the prisoners and recovery for the blind, to release the oppressed, to proclaim the year of the Lord's favor.' Then he rolled up the scroll, gave it back and sat down. The eyes of everyone were fastened on him and he began to say to them, 'Today this scripture is fulfilled in your hearing.'" Luke 4:17-21**

Jesus continued teaching and performing miracles among the throngs of people who gathered and followed Him daily. Some of the teachings are challenging but Christians believe this scripture, **"With man this is impossible, but with God all things are possible." Matt.19: 26** Lenten luncheons in a different church each week in the community are times for Christians to unite and invite seekers of God to hear about Jesus. It is a life or death matter for the unsaved. They need hope and Christians have it to share. Start praying for the lost to trust Jesus now.

REPENTANCE

The season of Lent is devoted to repentance. This is most important because sin separates us from a relationship with God. It goes way back to Adam and Eve in the Garden of Eden. By starting there, we are keeping the main thing the main thing. The fall of man in the Garden (sin) requires a sacrificial offering for the forgiveness of sin. In Old Testament days each Jewish family was required to bring the best lamb or goat to Passover. The High Priest of each Jewish tribe could then forgive this family's sin for the past year. Repent means to turn away from sin, to be sorry for what you have done and to promise to not do it again. The process was: High Priest orders the lamb or goat to be slaughtered, Priest enters the Holy of Holies and advances to the "Arc of the Covenant." The Arc is where the mercy seat of God is located. He places the blood of the lamb on the mercy seat which absolves the sin for the past year. No one except the Priest was allowed to enter the Holy of Holies. This was an action of repentance and required by law for all Jews. New Testament Christians know that there is no forgiveness of sin without accepting Christ and His blood shed on the Cross of Calvary!

Christians no longer live under law because Jesus set believers free from the law of sin and death when He bled and died on the Cross. After three days, Jesus arose from the dead so that we might have eternal life with Him in heaven. He, the Son of God, obeyed His Father, took upon Himself our sin and cancelled hell for us. He paid our sin debt in full. We, believers in Jesus, are now under grace. Christians live under grace "in Christ" to bring Him glory as we love Him and serve Him. Christian repentance is very different from Old Testament times. Jesus Christ asks us to confess to Him our sin and turn from it. **"This righteousness from God comes through faith in Jesus Christ to all who believe. There is no difference, for all have sinned and fall short of the glory of God, and we are justified freely by His grace through redemption that came by Christ Jesus." Romans 3:22-23. "If we confess our sin, He is faithful and just and will forgive our sin and purify us from all unrighteousness." 1 John 1:9.** He always hears our heart-felt repentant prayers and responds with forgiveness and cleansing. Some sin we will gain victory over in our lifetime. Some sin, we will not. Through confession, humility and turning away from sin, practicing repentance, receiving His forgiveness and His love, we will also receive mercy. We will live a victorious life as forgiven sinners; and as God's children. Christian repentance is a change of heart, hopefully followed by changed behavior. It is growing in grace to glorify God, the Father, God, the Son and God, the Holy Spirit alive in us. We often refer to these three persons of the Godhead as The Trinity.

During Lent we make heart-felt changes to love God in new and better ways to bring Him glory. We use words like "consecration," maybe with prayer and fasting to draw closer to God; "Introspection," taking an inventory of our motivation and sincerity for loving and serving God. Admitting to ourselves and others that we need more of God and cannot live a righteous life without a close, personal relationship with Jesus. He promises this gift, the Holy Spirit, if we will trust Him by faith for everything. Salvation is a miracle for all believers! Tell Him you love Him because He first loved you and paid your sin debt in full by His blood shed on the Cross.

Jesus, Keep Me Near the Cross

1. Je - sus, keep me near the cross, There a pre - cious foun - tain;
2. Near the cross, a trem - bling soul, Love and mer - cy found me;
3. Near the cross! O lamb of God, Bring its scenes be - fore me;
4. Near the cross! I'll watch and wait, Ho - ping, trus - ting e - ver;

Free to all, a heal - ing stream, Flows from Cal - v'ry's moun - tain.
There the Bright and Mor - ning Star Shed His beams a - round me.
Help me walk from day to day With its sha - dow o'er me.
Till I reach the gol - den strand, Just be - yond the ri - ver.

In the cross, in the cross Be my glo - ry e - ver,

Till my ran - somed soul shall find Rest be - yond the ri - ver.

Text: Fanny J. Crosby, 1820-1915
Tune: William H. Doane, 1832-1915

76 76 Refrain
NEAR THE CROSS
www.hymnary.org/text/jesus_keep_me_near_the_cross

Go to Dark Gethsemane

1. Go to dark Geth - se - ma - ne, You who feel the temp - ter's pow'r;
2. Fol - low to the judg - ment hall; View the Lord of life ar - raigned;
3. Cal - v'ry's mourn - ful moun - tain climb There' a - do - ring at His feet,
4. Ear - ly has - ten to the tomb Where they laid , his breath - less clay;

Your Re - dee - mer's con - flict see; Watch with Him one bit - ter hour;
O the worm - wood and the gall! O the pangs His soul sus - tained!
Mark the mi - ra - cle of time, God's own sac - ri - fice com - plete:
All is so - li - tude and gloom; Who hath ta - ken Him a - way?

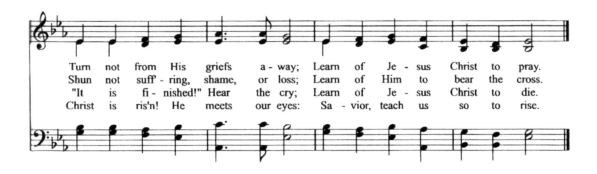

Turn not from His griefs a - way; Learn of Je - sus Christ to pray.
Shun not suff' - ring, shame, or loss; Learn of Him to bear the cross.
"It is fi - nished!" Hear the cry; Learn of Je - sus Christ to die.
Christ is ris'n! He meets our eyes: Sa - vior, teach us so to rise.

Text: James Montgomery, 1771-1854
Tune: Richard Redhead, 1820-1901

77 77 77
READHEAD 76
www.hymnary.org/text/go_to_dark_gethsemane

The great egret is a member of the Heron family, nests in trees, loves marshes and eats fish, frogs, snakes and crayfish. He builds a nest on a platform of sticks in trees. Three to five pale blue-green eggs are laid on the sticks. Egrets are stalking hunters when wading through water in the marshes and often find a fish for lunch there. Hunters nearly made these beautiful creatures extinct because they killed egrets to sell the white plumage. In the late 19th century, these plumes were added to hats and cherished by hat makers for high society events. Egrets fly slowly but powerfully with just two wing beats per second. Their cruising speed is around 25 miles per hour. The pristinely white Great egret gets very dressed up for the breeding season. A patch of skin on his face turns neon green, and long plumes grow from his back. In this photo he is in full breeding display. He is picking out old dead feathers and making his appearance as beautiful as possible. He is looking magnificent and very athletic today. Cleaning, sorting and discarding unwanted feathers is called preening.

"Therefore, I urge you, brothers, in view of God's mercy, to offer your bodies as living sacrifices, holy and pleasing to God – this is your spiritual act of worship. Do not conform any longer to the pattern of this world, but be transformed by the renewing of your mind. Then you will be able to test and approve what God's will is – his good, pleasing and perfect will."
Romans 12: 1-2

This egret is instinctively pleasing God by doing this preening to be a more pleasing and attractive bird. God-given instincts lead this egret to take good care of himself especially now that he has his breeding plumage. In this scripture, God is reminding us, His children, that taking good care of our body and mind is like the egret preening. When we open the bible and read, we stimulate our mind to think about our Lord and His plan for our lives. When we renew our mind in the word, drawing closer to God, it is pleasing God. He calls it our spiritual act of worship. He created us to know Him, love Him, worship Him, and bring Him glory in all we do. He is our Lord and Savior, our perfect friend, our Abba Father, Daddy, so very dear.

Prayer: Lord God, I love to worship you all through the year. You are worthy of all my praise whether I am celebrating Christmas, Lent or just any ordinary day. Thank you for the scriptures that renew my mind; to learn more about what it means to repent; to turn away from sin and to be cleansed from unrighteousness. I love your bird families in nature because I'm learning a lot about preening in my own life. Forgive me when I choose sin knowing that it is wrong. For today, Lord, I'm asking for your good, pleasing and perfect will. Thank you that during Lent I can grow closer to you with prayer and fasting. I want more of your peace and joy in my daily life. As I learn from your natural world, also help me understand your spiritual world and how they intertwine. Thank you, Lord, you are an amazing God, an awesome God, and a loving and personal God; the God who first loved me so I can love you, myself and others, in Jesus' precious name to glorify Him during this season of Lent, Holy Week and Easter, Amen.

Who doesn't love to watch a hummingbird? Oh, how sweet it is! Many enjoy seeing these very small beauties at their artificial feeders with fresh sugar water. The red feeders, because of their color, do attract this precious flower bed friend. In your flower garden, he will stop at tubular red flowers such as salvia, bee balm, petunias and trumpet creeper. He is constantly in motion and the only hummingbird that breeds east of the Mississippi River from Southern Canada to the Gulf Coast. He makes it all the way to the tropics where he winters and rarely stops at the Gulf Coast. He sings with mouse-like twittering squeaks. The best part is his mating performance. Just visualize these creative dance moves! First, the female sits quietly on a perch while he goes into his God-given dancing display. Starting a pendulum move and then swinging in a wide arc, buzzing loudly with each dip, he knows she is impressed because God made her that way. She does not have free will like humans do; so, for him, it is a win-win. His wings continually hum in this courtship display. These birds are a loving example of God's perfect plan to procreate His magnificent creation that He spoke into being.

"In that day I will make a covenant for them with the beasts of the field, the birds of the sky and the creatures that move along the ground. Bow and sword and battle I will abolish from the land, so that all may lie down in safety. I will betroth you to me forever; I will betroth you in righteousness and justice, with love and compassion. I will betroth you in faithfulness, and you will acknowledge the Lord."

Hosea 2: 18-20

This scripture was written by the Prophet Hosea around 722 BC, 700+ years before Christ was born. Hosea had marriage problems; his wife was unfaithful to him. He is giving us a description of the second coming of Christ. Jesus, our Bridegroom, comes back to earth for His Bride, the church of believers. The example above of the faithful and loving hummingbirds is today's sermon in a second. She, the church of believers, is patiently waiting for Jesus to fulfill His promise in this scripture to return to earth for His Bride. Our Bridegroom, Jesus, longs for a loving, intimate relationship with His Bride, each believer in His church. Betroth means "to bind with a promise to marry." Yes, we, His Bride, are married to Jesus forever! In heaven we will celebrate together "the Wedding Supper of the Lamb." **Revelation 19: 9**

Prayer: Lord God, my Bridegroom forever, you will never leave me or forsake me. This scripture above is as precious as this gifted, humble and colorful hummingbird on my left. Everything you have made is not only good but the indwelling Holy Spirit is an indescribable gift that is my invitation to the Wedding Supper of the Lamb. I love you, Lord and love your wisdom in the Bible. Please give me, daily, a teachable Spirit with more passion to learn more about you. In your presence is the fullness of joy, in Jesus' name and for His sake, Amen.

The tundra regions are found in the Arctic and on the tops of mountains where the climate is cold and windy; where very little rain falls. The land is covered with snow much of the year, but summer does bring a bouquet of wildflowers on the ground. "Freddie Finch" is foraging for seeds on the ground under the snow. When he finds black oil sunflower seeds, he is excited; his favorite meal! This songbird may fly to Denali today, the highest peak in the Alaskan mountains, where he has built his nest on the slopes. He will locate his breeding nest tucked tightly into the cliff side and settle down for a short winter nap. Freddie's remote breeding site keeps all humans from his awareness of the human race. This reminds us of the great grey owl, who lives so far from civilization that they are not afraid of humans. No contact, no worry! But if a human gets close, Freddie is fearless and allows people to approach. Thank you, Freddie, for letting our photographer close enough to record this wonderful event. The gray-crowned rosy Finches also love to live on the Alaskan Islands; however, these Islands are remote and not so easy to get to. This songbird is at peace whether in a blinding snowstorm or if there are very high winds bending the trees to the ground.

"Therefore, since we have been justified through faith, we have peace with God through our Lord Jesus Christ, through whom we have gained access by faith into this grace in which we now stand. And we rejoice in the hope of the glory of God."
Romans 5: 1-2

Does God love and watch Freddie and all his friends in the tundra region? Are not five sparrows sold for two pennies? Yet not one of them is forgotten by God. **Luke 12: 6.** How much more does He love you, His child? How much more does He want you to live in peace through our Lord Jesus Christ? Freddie lives a simple and faithful life. He is at peace no matter what is going on around him. The goodness of God supplies everything Freddie needs including peace in all circumstances. We need the word of God because we have been given free will to do, say, wound, destroy, anger, hate, love or reject anything or anyone we want to! **"Faith comes by hearing the message and the message is heard through the word of Christ." Romans 10: 17.** Faith in Jesus Christ is a decision made in the heart of a person who wants to stop worrying, hating, wounding, rejecting what God has made and what God has planned for His children. When you make God choices, He receives the glory! You receive His peace and if you continue in faith, you keep His peace forever; just like Freddie Finch and all of his Finch friends in the avian kingdom.

Prayer: Lord God, my Prince of peace, my Shelter in the storm, I want more of your word in my life. Lead me to bible studies so I can get to know you more and love you the way you deserve to be loved. I know I have much to learn but just receiving your peace today and knowing more about your love is changing my heart, thank you, in Jesus' name, Amen.

RED BELLIED WOODPECKER – *clinging to a Birch stump*   *Melanerpes carolinus*
Duanesburg, New York   Common

Meet "Red Ed" who is a forest dweller and loves to cling to trees. Today, all he could find was this white birch stump; but he is contented except for the cold weather and icy berries. He likes wood-boring beetles, grasshoppers, ants, acorns, beechnuts and wild fruits. He stores food so as not to run out in bad weather or hard times. Red Ed is happy when he finds a backyard feeder where the food is so easy to get at. You could even find him stealing nectar from a hummingbird feeder. God gave him a barbed tip on his tongue and he can stick his tongue out nearly 2 inches past the end of his beak. God also gave him sticky bird spit to make it easier to snatch prey from deep crevices. He can wedge large nuts into bark crevices and then whack them into manageable pieces using his beak. Red Ed has one enemy. If the European starlings find Red Ed in any nest, his own or a neighbor's, the starlings with take over and invade Red Ed's nest and area. As many as half of all Red-bellied woodpecker nests get invaded by starlings. Mom and dad share the nest for incubation. Males are commonly on the nest at night. Mom takes her turn during the day.

**"The thief comes to steal and kill and destroy but I (Jesus) have
come that they may have life and have it to the full."
John 10: 10**

There is some common ground here between humans and Red Ed and his family. We both store food so we never run out. Red Ed and his mate sacrifice their time to find food in the forest for their family. Many humans have jobs to provide the money to buy food to keep the family healthy. Our bodies need care and protection from harmful things just like the red-bellies. Their enemy is the starling and humans have Satan, the devil and other names for the enemy of all humans. So, God asks us to keep our bodies healthy and holy so we can worship Him. Red Ed gets a good night's sleep so he can go out and find food for the family in the morning. Red Ed's mate gets her rest during the day as she sits on the eggs. Isn't God's plan just so perfect for His creation? It truly is amazing how nature and human life are synced so both can prosper and glorify God together. How are you doing in the area of living your life to the full for Jesus?

Prayer: Lord God, I offer my body as a living sacrifice today. I want to be holy as you are holy. Your mercy, I do not get what I deserve, is so important to me; also important is staying strong, disease free and practicing good health habits. I want to give you true and loving worship to bring you glory; forgive me when I fail to do your will and then please get me back on your right path. Lord, your Red-bellied woodpeckers have such beautiful bodies, thank you for them, and thank you for your love that sustains me through good health and days of not such good health, in Jesus' name, Amen.

What does it mean to be "comically tame?" Maybe "Bruce the Spruce" is friendly around strangers or perhaps he does a funny dance to entertain his visitors. We don't know unless we have a chance to view him in his mature coniferous setting. However, one author says that Bruce the Spruce's antics have given him a less than flattering name. He is called "fool hen!" Let's just say that he does "stand-up comedy!" He is displaying in this photo. Notice his bright red eyebrow comb. That is a sign that he is going into his comic act to impress the flock that has assembled around his stage. He makes swishes and whooshes with his tail. The whooshes come when he suddenly fans his tail open like a person of the past might have snapped open a fan. As he struts around, he appears to wobble a bit. When he is hungry, he feeds on buds, seeds, needles and insects. This kind of diet makes him unpalatable to many hunters. Another name given to Bruce the Spruce besides "fool hen" is "swamp partridge."

"I thought in my heart, 'Come now, I will test you with pleasure to find out what is good.' But that proved to be meaningless. 'Laughter,' I said, 'is foolish. And what does pleasure accomplish'? I tried cheering myself with wine, and embracing folly, my mind still guiding me with wisdom. I wanted to see what was worthwhile for men to do under heaven during the few days of their lives."
Ecclesiastes 2: 1-3

Ecclesiastes studies the meaning of life. The "Teacher" looks at wisdom, pleasure, work, power, riches, religion, and other things. All of these have some value and are useful at the proper time and place; but they have lasting value only if God is at the center of man's life. Reverence and respect for God and a real devotion in serving God are most important in bringing meaning to life. Without God, the "Teacher" says, "everything is meaningless." The spruce grouse was created by God. God is the Creator of everything good and He loves and owns everything. Some things in life are funny, some are sad, some are beautiful and some are not. But what is important is that everything God has made has value and we have to read Ecclesiastes realizing that the author was searching for all the wrong things in all the wrong places. He has a skewed view of life. The "Teacher" is right when he says, **"Only if God is at the center does anything have value."** 1Timothy 4: 8 The spruce grouse can entertain and lift our spirits. How are you doing today? "Down" in spirit or "Up" in Holy Spirit love and power?

Prayer: Lord God, Creator of all valuable things, I always want you to be the center of my life. You bring true pleasure and give me Godly wisdom; you even make me laugh often. I don't know when I will be finished here on earth; but one thing is for sure, your timing, Lord, is always perfect. All the things you have made are valuable and I can't thank you enough for all that you did on Calvary's Cross so I can live as a forgiven child of God. Help me to add value to the lives of others today as I put you in the center of my life, in Jesus' name, Amen.

BALD EAGLE – an "eagle eye" on the prize

Alaska

Haliacetus leucosephalus

Uncommon

The expression "eagle eye" was first used back around 1598. The definition of "eagle eye" is: the ability to see or observe keenly, keep close watch. This stately fellow on his solid rock is keeping an eagle eye on the fast-moving water. A fresh fish is his "take out" main course when he is hungry. He will snatch the fish from near the top of the water with his strong and sharp talons. The eagle can convey the powers and messages of the spirit; it is man's connection to the divine because it flies higher than any other bird in the avian world. The eagle is symbolic of the importance of honesty and truthful principles. They create massive nests of sticks piled high before the female lays 2-3 white eggs. Often, they will continue building layer by layer until the nest is extremely high. Of course, that happens after the young leave home.

"Consider the ravens: They do not sow or reap; they have no storeroom or barn; yet God feeds them. And how much more valuable you are than birds!"
Luke 12: 24

Some researchers say that the eagle can be man's connection to the divine. These are lovely thoughts about the eagle and certainly God does love and feed the eagles by supplying fish in the waters. God's economical plan for birds and all living things is spectacular to say the least but God gave man a heart that can either live in darkness or receive God's light. Sin is man's problem. Repentance for sin by way of confession will change a dark human heart into the glorious light of connection to God. Believers have received not only God's light but also God's unconditional love. Knowing that God loves you is to know you are of great value to God here on earth. Birds are of value to God or He probably would not have created them. Who doesn't love hearing flocks of birds singing in the spring time? The beautiful coloring on birds in flight acts like a paint brush on the sky's canvas. We enjoy God's creation in the out of doors and so does God. God created man to love Him, to love each other and to love ourselves. God has made unconditional love His main theme here on earth. You are made in His image and a very valuable part of His plan. He loves all of mankind unconditionally. He has a wonderful plan for you. His love for you is unstoppable, do you receive it? He bled on the Cross for you. Let's thank Him now and ask to receive His love in our prayer today.

Prayer: Lord God, thank you for giving me a life of love. Your love for me convinces me that I am very valuable to you. Thank you for beautiful birds like the eagles. I love hearing and seeing birds as they make their colorful flight with singing across the sky. I want to spend more time with you, Lord. I want to hear your loving voice and discern your plan for my day. Now, I am going to be still and know that you are God. Resting in my chair, I love your presence and enjoy your still, small voice. Lord, your servant is listening. Please see my heart and refill it with your love, in the name of Jesus, the name that is above all names, Amen.

"Elmer Eagle" named after another famous father, is showing so much self-control as he makes his way back to the eaglets in the nest. Elmer is hungry but his first responsibility is to feed his family. He is carrying his prize home in his mouth and will share it. Yes, he is the eagle on the solid rock on the last page. Using his eagle eye was what gave him success on his fishing expedition. The goodness of God has made all this possible for Elmer and his new family. He instinctively knows the will of God today and he is doing just that. Elmer developed his white head feathers when he became mature at the age of 4-5 years old. Not all Bald Eagles are as caring and generous as Elmer. Rather than doing their own fishing, some eagles go after the catch of their neighbors. They will harass an Osprey until his meal drops out of his talons and then the eagle will drop down and swoop it up in midair. He is what you might call "an open-air pirate." Let's just say that there are eagles who have "lazy" eagle eyes and instead of getting their own prize they steal from a neighbor. No, it is not right to steal.

"Forget the former things; do not dwell on the past. See, I am doing a new thing! Now it springs up; do you not perceive it? I am making a way in the desert and streams in the wasteland. The wild animals honor me, the jackals and the owls, because I provide water in the desert and streams in the wasteland, to give drink to my people, my chosen, the people I formed for myself that they may proclaim my praise."

Isaiah 43: 18-21

When we have been treated unjustly, God wants justice but if it is a small offense with little or no harm done, God reminds us to not dwell on it but move on, forgive and forget. But if some harm has been done then we can pursue justice. We should be treated justly and then we can move on. Forgiving is hard but it helps everybody involved and gives God praise. The Osprey do not forgive or forget. They instinctively know how to stay away from the stealers. It is so easy for birds to move on to another state or territory if they have to; not so easy for humans. God is also reminding us that we can always look forward to the new thing He is doing and avoid getting stuck in the past. When we listen for God's wisdom, give thanks and praise God, we show God how much we love Him and trust His love, provision and protection.

Prayer: Lord God, thank you for the example of injustice when a bird steals another bird's meal. Trusting you, God, means waiting until you provide for my needs. I am learning to wait for your answers. Trusting you also means that I may not need what I think I need. I wait, look for your new direction forward and praise you for whatever answer you send me. Your timing, Lord, is always perfect. You are never early or never late with your answers. I am grateful that I don't have to ever get stuck again. Can't wait to see what comes next! It will be very exciting and I trust you will help me discern each step forward. Thank you for helping me grow closer to you, in the loving name of Jesus Christ, my Lord and Savior, Amen.

PINE SISKIN – "I got here first!"   Spinus pinus – in steep decline
BOREAL CHICKADEE – "But it's my pew!"   Poecile hudsonicus – uncommon
Alaska

A Pine siskin is a small, heavily streaked finch with deeply notched tail and sharply pointed bill. Flocks of these tiny birds may love your thistle feeder one winter and not come back the next year. This siskin ranges widely and erratically across the continent each winter in response to seed crops. They love to cling to the end of conifer branches, even upside down, to feed on pine cones. Boreal means up north or from the northern region. The Boreal chickadee leads a sedentary lifestyle and is a hard species for most bird watchers to see without a far trip north to Canada or Alaska. This Boreal, brown-capped chickadee, is a song bird who sometimes travels with his kinglet friends. Like most chickadees, the Boreal hides food regularly, known as cashing (hiding). This is vital for winter survival in the boreal regions.

"Do not let any unwholesome talk come out of your mouths, but only what is helpful for building others up according to their needs, that it may benefit those who listen."
Ephesians 4: 29

In this photo there may be a bit of a disagreement about who owns the perch that is so beautifully decorated with pine cones. The dialog at the top of this page suggests that the song birds are arguing about ownership. Has this ever happened to you? Or it could be about a place waiting in line? Or it could be about, as our bird friends suggest, finding a church pew to sit in for worship? Some of God's children have endured a nasty frown or an unwanted word or two when trying to get seated for worship. Hopefully, there will be gracious ushers next time who will ask you, "Where would you like to sit?" Since God owns everything, can we just be thankful that there is at least one empty seat and we found it without upsetting anyone? Or can we just be grateful that a new face has chosen our church for worship today? It is true, some people think they own everything. No, God owns it all. It is as basic as your next breath. "God gives life and God takes life away." **Job 1:21**. How dependent are you on God for every breath? How grateful are you for everything good in your life? How about your relationship with Jesus? Is it growing? Does your relationship with Jesus help you value others and build others up?

Prayer: Lord God, Creator and Owner of everything good, forgive me when I think I own something, everything is yours. I am so thankful that you have provided for all my needs and that I have a wonderful life on this earth because of your generosity. I am grateful for my salvation, for the Holy Spirit that you abundantly give to those who ask. Your blood shed on the Cross of Calvary for forgiveness of sin is one of the best gifts because when I mess up, confess and repent, I am forgiven. How amazing and precious is your unconditional love for all of your creation. I am so thankful for our intimate relationship, I love you, Lord, yesterday, today, tomorrow and forever, in Jesus' name and for His glory for all of eternity, Amen.

Hosanna, Loud Hosanna

1 Ho - san - na, loud ho - san - na the lit - tle chil - dren sang;
2 From Ol - i - vet they fol - lowed mid an ex - ul - tant crowd,
3 "Ho - san - na in the high - est!" That an - cient song we sing,

through pil - lared court and tem - ple the love - ly an - them rang.
the vic - tory palm branch wav - ing, and chant - ing clear and loud.
for Christ is our Re - deem - er, the Lord of heaven, our King.

To Je - sus, who had blessed them, close fold - ed to his breast,
The Lord of earth and heav - en rode on in low - ly state,
O may we ev - er praise him with heart and life and voice,

the chil - dren sang their prais - es, the sim - plest and the best.
nor scorned that lit - tle chil - dren should on his bid - ding wait.
and in his bliss - ful pres - ence e - ter - nal - ly re - joice.

Text: Jennette Threlfall, 1873
Tune: *Gesangbuch*, Wittenberg, 1784

76 76 D
ELLACOMBE
www.hymnary.org/text/hosanna_loud_hosanna_the_little_children

'Tis Finished! The Messiah Dies

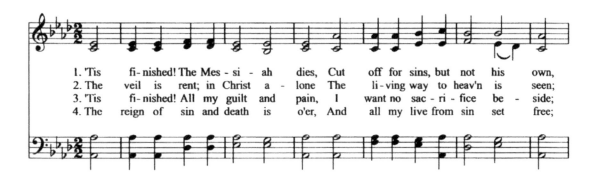

1. 'Tis fi-nished! The Mes-si-ah dies, Cut off for sins, but not his own,
2. The veil is rent; in Christ a-lone The li-ving way to heav'n is seen;
3. 'Tis fi-nished! All my guilt and pain, I want no sac-ri-fice be-side;
4. The reign of sin and death is o'er, And all my live from sin set free;

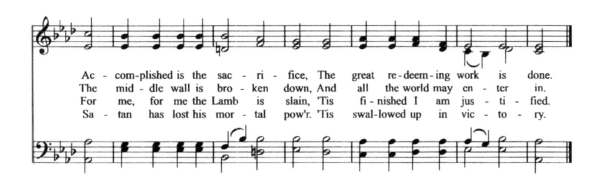

Ac-com-plished is the sac-ri-fice, The great re-deem-ing work is done.
The mid-dle wall is bro-ken down, And all the world may en-ter in.
For me, for me the Lamb is slain, 'Tis fi-nished I am jus-ti-fied.
Sa-tan has lost his mor-tal pow'r. 'Tis swal-lowed up in vic-to-ry.

REST FOR THE WEARY

"Come to me, all you who are weary and burdened, and I will give you rest. Take my yoke upon you and learn from me, for I am gentle and humble in heart, and you will find rest for your souls. For my yoke is easy and my burden is light."

Matthew 11: 28-30

Text: Charles Wesley, 1707-1788
Tune: William B. Bradbury, 1816-1868

88 88
OLIVE'S BROW
www.hymnary.org/text/tis_finished_the_messiah_dies

PART 2

HOLY WEEK
SHOUTS OF PRAISE for the "KING OF LOVE" on PALM SUNDAY

Holy Week starts with the Triumphal entry of Jesus through the streets of Jerusalem. This is one week before Easter. This Sunday is known as **PALM SUNDAY** with large crowds following Jesus, praising him and waving palm branches in celebration of the weeks coming events. He is honored by His followers as "King of the Jews" but that did not make the Jewish authorities happy! They started plotting against Him. His followers were filled with joy as He was on His way to the Temple. Here are selected scriptures to help us celebrate Palm Sunday.

"As they approached Jerusalem and came to Bethany at the Mount of Olives, Jesus sent two of his disciples, saying to them, 'Go to the village ahead of you, and just as you enter it, you will find a colt tied there, which no one has ever ridden. Untie it and bring it here. If anyone asks you, why are you doing this? tell him, The Lord needs it and will send it back here shortly.'" Mark 11: 1-3 "When they brought the colt to Jesus and threw their cloaks over it, he sat on it. Many people spread their cloaks on the road, while others spread branches they had cut in the fields. Those who went ahead and those behind shouted; 'HOSANNA! Blessed is he who comes in the name of the Lord! Blessed is the coming kingdom of our Father David! HOSANNA in the Highest!' "Mark 11: 7-10 "The next day, on reaching Jerusalem again, Jesus entered the temple area and began driving out those who were buying and selling there. He overturned the tables of the money changers and the benches of those selling doves, and would not allow anyone to carry merchandise through the temple courts. And as he taught them, he said, 'is it not written: My house will be called a house of prayer for all nations? You have made it a den of robbers.'" Mark 11:15-17

Christians worship on Palm Sunday with special music, spring flowers, waving of palm branches and the reading of these scriptures. Sometimes Christians celebrate **HOLY THURSDAY** with a Seder meal, a Jewish tradition during Passover. Jesus not only served the first communion to his disciples that **HOLY THURSDAY** but He also demonstrated His humility as the servant of all. He wrapped a towel around His waist and washed the feet of the disciples and said, **"For even the Son of Man did not come to be served, but to serve, and to give His life as a ransom for many." Mark 10: 45** Judas left the meeting early and we all know why! Jesus served the last supper, bread and wine, to His disciples with directions about the future when we would do the same in remembrance of Him. These consecrated elements become the body and blood of our Lord. We partake in His suffering and His death, our death to self, when we take these elements. We do this to glorify God and to live our lives in close communion with Him. In the Methodist tradition we proclaim: **"Christ has died, Christ is risen, and Christ is coming again!"** Appropriately, we call this "Communion" in the worship service. Next is from the Gospel of Mark and Paul's Letter to the Corinthians, some of the most powerful words and acts of kindness from Jesus to us, His believers.

"It is one of the twelve, Jesus replied. The Son of Man will go just as it is written about him. But woe to that man who betrays the Son of Man! It would be better for him if he had not been born." Mark 14:21

"And when He had given thanks, He broke it (bread) and said, "Take, eat; this is my body broken for you; do this in remembrance of Me." In the same manner after supper, He gave thanks, took the cup, saying, "This cup is the new covenant in my blood. This do, as often as you drink it, in remembrance of Me." 1 Corinthians11: 24-25 (NKJV)

"I tell you the truth, I will not drink again of the fruit of the vine until
that day when I drink it anew in the kingdom of God. When they had sung
a hymn, they went out to the Mt. of Olives." Mark 14: 25-26

The next day is the first "**GOOD FRIDAY**" in the miraculous on-going story of Christianity. Jesus is arrested, beaten, brutalized, whipped, and faces a criminal death on a wooden cross. This is referred to as crucifixion, the most brutal way to cause death to a human. The nails pierced his hands and feet. As He bled profusely, Jesus became the sinless "Lamb of God." Christians lament what Jesus had to go through as the sinless Son of God. Our Father in heaven sent His one and only Son to take on all the sins of the world. Believers receive God's salvation; His forgiveness for sin, His unconditional love with life in the Holy Spirit forever. This is **"DIVINE LOVE"** with heaven our destiny!

This is a good day for the human race, usually a holiday from work, but for Christians, a day of sorrow and repentance. On Good Friday, Christians meditate on scripture, pray with fasting, out of gratitude for what Jesus Christ has done for us. He took the whipping, piercing, bleeding, shame and rejection that we deserved.

Jesus was fully man and fully God. Jesus sacrificed His human life to set us free from sin and death. He was only 33 years old. Jesus did not want this cup of death on a painful cross of nails. He asked His Father in Heaven to take this cup away but the answer was no! The sky went black for three hours when our Lord was slowly dying. He ended it by telling His Father in heaven, "into your hands, Father, I give up My Spirit" and "It is finished." Man knows no greater love in all the universe. Here are some scriptures about the death of our Savior. You will want to read all of the Gospels, Matthew, Mark, Luke and John when you have time during Lent.

"At the sixth hour darkness came over the whole land until the ninth hour. And at the ninth hour Jesus cried out in a loud voice, *'Eloi, Eloi, lama sabachthani?'* - Which means, 'My God, my God, why have you forsaken me?' When some of those standing near heard this, they said, 'Listen, he is calling Elijah.' One man ran, filled a sponge with wine vinegar, put it on a stick, and offered it to Jesus to drink. 'Now leave him alone. Let's see if Elijah comes to take him down,' he said. With a loud cry, Jesus breathed his last. The curtain of the temple was torn in two from the top to bottom. And when the centurion, who stood there in front of Jesus, heard his cry and saw how he died, he said, 'Surely this man was the Son of God!' "Mark 15: 33-39

No one in all the world has ever loved you like Jesus loves you. He died a sinless death so you might know Him, love Him, serve Him and spend eternity in heaven with Him. My friend, there is no greater love; so, accept Jesus into your heart and live in peace with Him here and in eternity in heaven. Yes, this is the best day of your life if you know Jesus as Savior and Lord. A simple prayer from your heart to His heart is all it takes. End your prayer of confession as a sinner with "now fill me with your Holy Spirit so I can hear your voice, receive your love and peace daily." **We are saved by grace, (undeserved favor), and not by works lest any man should boast." Eph. 2: 9.** Many are not saved and now your testimony is very important to God. Tell someone that you are saved. Give your testimony to those who will listen. Continue to nurture your loving friendship with Jesus through bible reading and prayer. Start with the Gospel of John in the New Testament. Very soon Jesus will become your very best friend. Prayer is talking and listening to God. Live a life of prayer and praise and you will never be the same. This day remains good for non-believers because God is waiting with open arms for everyone to come to the knowledge and love of the finished work of Jesus on the Cross of Calvary. Everyday all over the world many are surrendering to God and starting a new life of praise, prayer and thanksgiving "in Christ." Welcome, Friend, we are sisters and brothers in the Lord. Praise His Holy name! He is faithful and His love endures forever. **Now, please hear my Pastor's heart in her Good Friday on-line message for 2020. (No worship service due to closed churches because of the coronavirus lock down – Covid-19 world-wide pandemic).**

"Today is Good Friday, 2020. There is a tradition that at the conclusion of the Good Friday service the sanctuary is "stripped." Everything of beauty is removed from the sanctuary. All that's left is the cross, draped in black cloth.

Today, more than any year I can remember, the church is stripped for Good Friday. We are stripped of many things that we associate with church. Stripped of the spiritual fellowship of brothers and sisters. Stripped of the ability to meet together in worship. Stripped of the traditions that we cherish. In the sanctuary, the chairs are empty. As Jesus hung nailed to the cross, he was stripped. Stripped of clothing. Stripped of dignity. Stripped of the acclaim of his many followers. Even stripped of his intimacy with his God. Ultimately, stripped of his very life. How do we, believers in Jesus, respond to this stripping? By letting God strip us as well. I write "letting God strip us" because I know that I cannot strip myself. Only God can put our hearts in a place where we are willing to be stripped.

Stripped of what? Our reliance on being together in order to worship God. Our belief that we are strong enough to handle things on our own. Our need to control our lives so that nothing can get in and hurt us.

Stripped of our pride............ Stripped of our affluence............ Stripped of our façade of goodness.

In the Garden of Gethsemane Jesus fell on his face and pleaded with God to have mercy on him. God answered "No", and Jesus went to the cross for the sins of the world. Today, this Good Friday, let us fall on our faces before God and plead for mercy.

Mercy for the church, for all the ways that we have failed to be the body of Christ in the world. For the times we have been more concerned about ourselves than about the hurting world around us. For the times we have thought we were better than the "sinners" outside our church doors. For the times we have allowed our traditions to keep us from doing new things and finding new ways to reach others for Christ.

Mercy for each of us as individuals for all the ways we have failed to be like Christ. Mercy for our nation and for the world that has turned away from God and thought we could save ourselves.

God, strip us of our sin…………God, have mercy on us………… God, forgive us.

Rev. Judy Humphrey-Fox, Pastor, Amsterdam United Methodist Church and

Restoration Ministry (Bilingual, Spanish/English), Amsterdam, New York

Later, Joseph of Arimathea asked Pilate for the body of Jesus. Now Joseph was a Disciple of Jesus, but secretly because he feared the Jews. With Pilate's permission, he came and took the body away. He was accompanied by Nicodemus, the man who earlier had visited Jesus at night. Nicodemus brought a mixture of myrrh and aloes, about seventy-five pounds. Taking Jesus body, the two of them wrapped it with the spices in strips of linen. This was in accordance with Jewish burial customs. At the place where Jesus was crucified, there was a garden, and in the garden a new tomb, in which no one had ever been laid. Because it was the Jewish day of Preparation and since the tomb was nearby, they laid Jesus there. The following is a prayer for salvation to receive Christ today:

Lord God, I need a relationship with you. Jesus, be my Savior and Lord. You are the sinless Son of God who died for me. I confess that I am a sinner and need your forgiveness. I understand that you are filling me with your Holy Spirit as a free gift to live inside me while I live out my life for you. I know that your blood shed for me on the Cross of Calvary was the supreme act of love that you did for all sinners. Now I am one of your beloved children called to love you, God, love myself and others with this same unconditional love. Thank you, Jesus, for your mercy and grace that was so unselfishly given on the Cross; your blood shed on Calvary has saved me, thank you, I am a forgiven sinner, your beloved child forever, in Jesus' name, Amen.

Members of the Amsterdam UMC begin their times of prayer together with: "**O God, we confess the blindness that is not even aware of sinning; the pride that dares not admit that it is wrong; the selfishness that can see nothing but its own will; the righteousness that knows no fault; the callousness that has ceased to care; the defiance that does not regret its own sins; the evasion that always tries to make excuses; the coldness of heart that is too hardened to repent. Give us at all times, eyes which are open to our faults; a conscience which is sensitive and quick to warn; a heart that cannot sin in peace, but is moved to regret and remorse. So, grant that being truly penitent we may be truly forgiven for your love is great enough to cover all sin; Through Jesus Christ our Lord, Amen.**" ……William Barclay in Prayers for the Christian Year – 1965, abebooks.com.

"Sunny," the singing warbler is sure enjoying himself this morning. He decided to join the buttercup choir and sing in harmony with them. Can you hear them? *"You are my sunshine, my only sunshine, you make me happy when skies are grey. You'll never know dear how much I love you, do not take my sunshine away!"* Wow! What a beautiful voice you have and thanks for singing with Sunny. His song, a bright, sweet refrain, is a familiar sound in the streamside willows and grassland edges. He nests from the Arctic Circle to Mexico and likes the tropical coastlines, too. Their open, cuplike nests are sometimes shared with the cowbirds; not because the warblers want to share but only because the cowbirds lay eggs in them as soon as the nest building is done. This unwanted intrusion has consequences for the cowbird. The warbler will then build a new floor over the cowbird eggs and lay more warbler eggs on top. In one case, pushy cowbird returned five times to lay more eggs in one nest. An even more persistent warbler built six layers of nest floor to cover the cowbird eggs! This sounds like a reality TV show that might be called, "Bird Brain Race," the first egg to hatch and survive is the winner!

"What shall we say, then? Shall we continue in sin, that grace may abound? God forbid! How shall we, that are dead to sin, live any longer there in?"
Romans 6: 1-2 (KJV)

The three-letter word, sin, is so often left out of sermons these days. Why is that? We will not answer that today but let's take a look at what's going on in this Bird Brain Race. The sin of using something that is not yours without permission is called stealing. And because it is happening over and over and over again is also: annoying, dangerous, stupid and infuriating to say the least! It's a warbler nest to start with so the perpetrators are the cowbirds. Now there is no law enforcement agencies in the bird world so that is why the craziness goes on and on. There is no way of stopping the fight to be the last bird to lay eggs on the highest floor of the nest. This would make a very funny video to show to friends along with the story line! However, problems like this do happen in the sinful world of the human race. Law enforcement has to be called often to end disputes or to arrest someone. But God went to the Cross of Calvary to pay our sin debt so we can live in a much safer place where we follow God's rules. God forgives sin but like the scripture says in Romans 6, believers are dead to sin and desire to live no longer doing what we know is wrong. When we need help from God we pray and listen and do the next right thing. God is glorified when we follow His rules. Let's thank God now:

Prayer: Lord God, because of your unconditional love at the Cross, I am a forgiven child of God. I want to hear your voice when I need help because you love me and I can't live a "set apart life" without your guidance. I'm glad I can learn lessons from nature and enjoy the beautiful songs of the birds and the amazing colors of the rainbow and sunsets. I praise you for all of creation and for my life in Christ that is full of joy, peace and your love, Amen.

This Puffin has a nickname, "Sea Parrot." Some parrots have beautiful coloring as does this puffin. He is very rarely seen from shore except when traveling in breeding colonies. He loves the rocky coasts and will build a nest in the crevices or under rocks. Sometimes he builds a burrow three- seven feet long. Both mom and dad puffin work together to excavate the nesting spot. She lays one white egg in the burrow in soft soil. They breed from the Canadian Maritimes south to Maine. They often keep the same mate year after year. In courtship, a male repeatedly flicks head up and back so that his bill points up. He continues these moves for a few minutes. Together they swing their bills sideways, clashing them together repeatedly. This comical-looking bird has another popular name, "Clown of the Sea." They are excellent divers and swimmers. Another wonderfully instinctive trait is; they both help feed the newborn puffins. They carry fish in their bill so their new born will grow and live a healthy life. After 38-44 days the newbies leave the nest at night and fly directly out to sea. Their unusual song and call is described as "chainsaw snores" and "sputtering snores." Lord God, when they leave the nest at night and fly alone directly out to sea, how do they know where to go?

"I have no need of a bull from your stall or of goats from your pens, for every animal of the forest is mine, and the cattle on a thousand hills. I know every bird in the mountains, and the creatures of the field are mine."

Psalm 50: 9-11

God's answer to our question above is in this scripture. The newborn puffin is God's puffin and he is flying out to sea being instinctively guided by God's plan for him. He will arrive safely because God loves him and has a good plan to make him a daddy someday. Maybe next year when we come back here, we can take a photo of this puffin's new family! Many songs have been written about the circle of life and rightly so. It is a miracle when anything is born into life on earth, whether human life or birds or animals. We, God's children, get to enjoy all the new life we see all around us. If God loves and protects His puffins, how much more will He love and protect you? **"Love does not delight in evil but rejoices with the truth. It always protects, always trusts, always hopes, and always perseveres." 1 Corinthians 13: 6-7**

Prayer: Lord God, thank you for creating and loving this adorable puffin and thank you for loving me, as needy as I am, you still love me. Your plan to fill the world with new life is so powerful. Abba Father, daddy so very dear, please save and protect the human babies in the womb that are being murdered before birth. Each one with a one-of-a-kind DNA, with God given giftedness and a profound purpose to live as a child of God to bring you, Lord, glory. Lord, I want and need more hope for tomorrow here in America. It is not the beautiful and peaceful place I grew up in. Help me, Lord, to be a faithful witness to point to your Cross and your blood shed there for the forgiveness of sin. Start with my heart, God, change me, Amen

The newborn chicks start out on mom's back but as they grow confident about their surroundings, they slide off to experience a new freedom. The call of the loon is like none other. This sound in nature so typifies the great American wilderness. The shivering cry cuts easily through fog awakening feelings in the human soul that go so deep they are never forgotten. Loons are water birds, only going ashore to mate and incubate eggs. Their legs are perfect for swimming but not so much for walking on land. Awkward does describe the loon trying to walk on land. Common loons are powerful, agile divers that catch small fish in fast underwater chases. They prefer water but typically come ashore only to nest. The fish dinner is consumed under the water – even though the fish is slippery, God gave the loon a special mouth and tongue that keep a firm hold on slippery fish. Besides swimming, they can fly very fast in the air. Migrating loons have been clocked at speeds of more than 70 mph. Think about this fact: loon parents and two chicks can eat about a half-ton of fish in 15 weeks- close to four months. Loons are master fishers! A loon can not only swim under water for long periods of time but they can also live a long time. A female Common loon was 29 years and 10 months old when she was spotted in Michigan in 2016. She had been banded in the same state in 1989.

"Finally, brothers and sisters, whatever is true, whatever is noble, whatever is right, whatever is pure, whatever is lovely, whatever is admirable – if anything is excellent or praiseworthy – think on these things."

Philippians 4: 8

Whatever is going on in your thoughts today, there is no excuse for being down or dreary right now! Start with this scripture and this loon photo. This Loon family is a beautiful picture of contentment, peace and purpose. So much of this meditation on the loon family is not just true but also noble, right, pure, lovely and admirable. Do you agree? If God takes such good care of His loon families, how much more will He provide for your needs? He loves His creatures in nature but He loves and values you so much more because He calls you His beloved child. Let's give God praise for who He is and give thanks for His redeeming work on the Cross. The power to overcome sin and eternity in hell is in the blood of Jesus. He promises that if you believe and trust Him you will spend eternity in heaven with Him.

Prayer: Lord God, your death on the Cross of Calvary is excellent and praiseworthy. Today I will continue to think on this meditation about the beautiful Loon family that you created. I thank you for giving me life in Christ and the gift of the Holy Spirit that makes everything good in my life possible. I realize that I am more valuable to you than these loons but they are magnificent and I am enjoying learning about them. My spirit is recharging and I am so glad we spent this time together. In your presence is the fullness of joy, thank you, Lord, all my praise is yours today and every day, in Jesus' name, Amen.

These two claves were probably born between March and April and are orange-red in color, earning them the nickname of "red dogs." After a few months, their hair will change to dark brown and their shoulder hump and horns begin to grow. You can judge a bison's mood by its tail. When it hangs down and swishes naturally, the bison is usually calm. If the tail is standing straight up, watch out! He or she may be ready to charge. No matter what a bison's tail is doing, remember that they are unpredictable and can charge at any moment. Every year there are unwanted accidents caused by people getting too close to these animals. When they are very young, like this pair, they are adorable but they will grow up like all of us do. It's great to love the bison, but love them from a distance. They will continue growing until reaching anywhere from 1,500 to 2,500 lbs. Several years ago, bison burgers appeared on the menu in restaurants and some people liked them but others said, "Where's the beef? They obviously preferred a hamburger.

"Therefore, we do not lose heart. Though outwardly we are wasting away, inwardly we are being renewed day by day. For our light and momentary troubles are achieving for us an eternal glory that far outweighs them all. So, we fix our eyes on not what is seen but on what is unseen. For what is seen is temporary, but what is unseen is eternal."
2 Corinthians 4: 16-18

It is true, by the time you are reading this page, these bison are growing older and as the scripture says, we are all wasting away the same as the bison. However, our loving and faithful God has called you, a human being, into relationship with Him. The bison, who you can see, will never be able to talk to God, who they can't see. They will live a natural life but God will know when the bison die and he will continue to enjoy these young guys as they grow year after year. God created everything and owns everything. You will, if you choose to, live a supernatural life in communication with God 24/7 as God promises. You can talk with God and He will hear you. You can renew your love for God by daily bible reading and prayer. No trouble will overtake you because Jesus is in charge of His children down here on earth. Enjoy the photo of the bison brothers but as soon as you turn the page, they are gone, unseen! Your great and wonderful God is always with you; so, focus on Jesus, who is unseen, but whose Spirit lives in you. Daily love, walk and talk with Him. He is eternal love; agape love, like no other kind of love and this love is only found in a personal relationship with Him, the Lover of your soul.

Prayer: Lord God, I have renewed my mind with this scripture and filled my heart with praise for who you are, Christ and Him crucified, my unseen, living, loving Lord! My heart is once again filled with thanksgiving for how much you love me. You are my Rock I stand on, you are my Lighthouse in the darkness, and you are my Anchor in the storm, I love you, Lord, and I want all unbelievers to know you and your love for them, in Jesus' name, Amen.

There are three species of swan in North America. Besides the Trumpeter, there are Tundra swans, living in the very northern cold climates and the Mute swan who breeds in freshwater marshes, ponds, lakes and rivers. There are about 34,000 Trumpeter swans in America and they are even on the increase as of 2015. This swan is known by his call, much like the sound of the French horn. Listen for a loud, full and deep sound. This swan is one of the heaviest flying birds in the world at around 30-35 lbs. Even though they are slowly increasing in numbers, they are still threatened by lead poisoning, collisions, illegal shootings and habitat loss. Something very special about the Trumpeter swan; he mates with a life-long female partner. Yes, this is instinctive and is the way God created their union. Their babies are called cygnets. The cygnets stay under the care of their parents for a full year.

"Marriage should be honored by all, and the marriage bed kept pure, for God will judge the adulterer and all the sexually immoral. Keep your lives free from the love of money and be content with what you have, because God has said, "Never will I leave you; never will I forsake you." Hebrews 13: 4-5

God's plan for love and marriage is the catalyst for creating and growing the many generations since Adam and Eve began the first family on earth. The beautiful swans are a reminder of God's plan for procreation to fill the world with beautiful families to bring glory to God. The swan mates for life as an example of God's faithful plan for all human family life and for starting new generations. We grow old together, we have grandchildren to enjoy and on and on the circle of life stretches. These events bring glory to God which is a Christian's purpose for living. Sex is reserved for the marriage bed of a man and woman who have made a covenant to be faithful to each other. Their union is a sacred covenant because that is God's plan. The world today is more than confused about sexuality. Today divorce is common; so is living together before marriage. Adultery, pedophilia and all other harmful, sexual sins have been rampant for too long. **Jesus said, "The enemy comes to rob, steal and destroy, but I have come that they might have life and have it more abundantly." John10: 10**

Prayer: Lord God, lover of my soul, thank you for giving me a soul mate who spent 41 years with me until his death in 2000. I am grateful for every one of those years, our two children and our two grandchildren. My hope is in you, Lord, come back soon and straighten out this confused planet and have the final say for the rest of eternity. Precious Jesus, I love you, want you and need you more than ever. Lord, please listen to my song, "*I love you, Lord, and I lift my voice to worship you; O, my soul rejoice! Take joy, my King, in what you hear; may it be a sweet, sweet sound in your ear.*" – Words by Laurie Klein, in Jesus' name, Amen.

Momma Brown Bear weighs in at around 1,500 lbs. Her cubs are only a few months old but this is the first time they wandered out of her sight. She is desperate and stands up on her hind paws to get a better look at the meadow up ahead. She doesn't see them so she gets worried because she knows how dangerous it is for the little cubs to encounter a predator without her protection. Again, she thinks, where are my crazy cubs? She is nearly 8 feet tall so she continually stands up and soon catches a familiar smell in the air. Brown Bears have a strong sense of smell and sure enough she follows her nose and hopes the smell she is picking up is her crazy cubs! Momma is called a sow and she is mostly a vegetarian and loves fruit when she finds it. These mature bears are dangerous if they are not treated with respect. Also, the cubs stay with momma for two-three years before they can go out on their own. The Grizzly bear is a subspecies of the Brown Bear in North America. Momma, who also is called a Grizzly bear, is now running toward that strong smell. She is going faster and faster and now she is out of sight! God, please help her find them!

"Be alert and of sober mind. Your enemy the devil prowls around like a roaring lion looking for someone to devour. Resist him, standing firm in the faith, because you know that the family of believers throughout the world is undergoing the same kind of sufferings."
1 Peter 5: 8-9

Momma Bear and humans have some of the same worries especially when our children could be in trouble, lost their way, are hungry with no food, or sick with no doctor. God has given us this scripture to help us get the help we need. We have an enemy, the devil, a liar, Satan, and the accuser of the brethren are some of his names. He does not want us to get well or have anything good happen to us in these scary times. However, God is in charge and He has all the goodness we can receive at any one time. God says, "Lean on your faith in Jesus; **He is with you and will never leave you or forsake you;" Hebrews 13: 5.** Getting through these hard times with faith is our testimony. We kept our faith alive and trusted Jesus. Everyone has these tough times. Our story of faith can lead another person to trust Christ for the first time.

Prayer: Lord God, my Protector, Great Physician and my reason for faith, you never fail to bring protection always in time to subside my fear and help me live in peace. I remember you said, "Get thee behind me, Satan;" and the enemy ran away and you were not bothered any longer. You, Lord, do have all the bases covered because you love everyone, all bears and all of creation. I'm quite sure you have protected Momma bear's crazy cubs; so, thank you for helping her today. Lord, your whole wide world doesn't know you yet but my prayer is that your Holy Spirit is drawing them now as I am in your presence lifting them up to you. As a believer, Lord, I know I must lovingly pray for the unsaved to be filled with hope in Christ, in the precious name of Jesus Christ and Him crucified, Amen.

BROWN BEAR FAMILY – *no longer lost!*   *Ursas arctos*

Alaska   *Common*

SURPRIZE! Momma found her cubs because she knew to follow their scent. God made her with a powerful sense of smell to find her children. This is a marvelous work of God. Thank you, Lord! The cubs were born with blond fur much lighter than Momma's darker brown. That color will change to darker when they get older. The green meadow and the blond fur tells us that it is springtime in Alaska. The cubs are newborn Brown/Grizzly bears and will stay with their Momma for two years as that is how long she nurses them. The bear family brings glory to God by living the life God made for them. They have instincts that show and tell them what they need to do to live in the beautiful meadows of Alaska. Remember that bears can be dangerous if they are not treated with respect. Alaska contains 98% of the U S Grizzly bear population. An estimated 30,000 Brown/Grizzly bears live in this state. About 1,450 are harvested by hunters every year. After two years, Momma bear will let them go off into the meadows and wilderness on their own to raise more generations of bears.

"God's voice thunders in marvelous ways; He does great things beyond our understanding. He says to the snow, 'fall on the earth,' and to the rain shower, 'Be a mighty downpour.' So that all men he has made may know his work, he stops every man from his labor." Job 37: 5-7

It is beyond our understanding to know God's thoughts and His ways. But we have so much proof of His great works on earth. Our Brown bear family is just one of His marvelous works. Sometimes we wonder why He does what He does. But we do not question Him because he is God and we are not! His children KNOW and LOVE Him. We know Him because He created us; gave us our first breath and when we believed, He filled us with the Holy Spirit. We love Him because He first loved us and suffered a horrifying death on the cross for our sin debt. We are His forgiven children. What a mighty work He did on the cross of Calvary for every believer. He literally shed His blood for us. He didn't stop there; but now we have eternal life in heaven with Him. He arose from the dead on the first Easter and we go to live with Him in heaven when He takes our last breath away. Always remember**: "God works all things together for good for those who love Him and are the called according to His purpose." Romans 8: 28.**

Prayer: Lord God, thank you for your many great works in nature that I enjoy every day of my life! Thank you for the word of God that helps me live a life of thanksgiving and love. Your word guides me and is like Momma bear's ability to smell her cubs in order to find them and get them back under her protection. You, Lord, have a marvelous plan for all of creation now and forever. I need your help to stay focused on you, God, and what this new day has in store for me. Your word says, "Draw close to God and He will draw close to you." James 4: 8. I must choose daily to fix my eyes on you and tune my ears to your voice, as I listen, hear you and obey. Thank you, Lord, for being my faithful Teacher, in the precious name that is above all names, the name of Jesus, Amen.

Crown Him with Many Crowns

1 Crown him with ma - ny crowns, the Lamb up - on his throne.
2 Crown him the Lord of life, who tri - umphed o'er the grave,
3 Crown him the Lord of love; be - hold his hands and side,
4 Crown him the Lord of years, the po - ten - tate of time,

Hark! how the heaven - ly an - them drowns all mu - sic but its own.
and rose vic - to - rious in the strife for those he came to save;
rich wounds, yet vi - si - ble a - bove, in beau - ty glo - ri - fied;
cre - a - tor of the rol - ling spheres, in - ef - fa - bly su - blime.

A - wake, my soul, and sing of him who died for thee,
his glo - ries now we sing who died and rose on high,
no an - gels in the sky can ful - ly bear that sight,
All hail, Re - dee - mer, hail! for thou hast died for me;

and hail him as thy match - less king through all e - ter - ni - ty.
who died e - ter - nal life to bring, and lives that death may die.
but down - ward bends their bur - ning eye at my - ste - ries so bright.
thy praise shall ne - ver, ne - ver fail through - out e - ter - ni - ty.

Text: Matthew Bridges (1800-1894) and
   Godfrey Thring (1823-1903)
Tune: George J. Elvey (1816-1893)

SMD
DIADEMATA
www.hymnary.org/text/crown_him_with_many_crowns

There Is a Fountain Filled with Blood

Text: William Cowper (1731-1800)
Tune: Traditional american melody;
arr. Lowell Mason (1792-1872)

86 86 66 86
CLEANSING FOUNTAIN
www.hymnary.org/there_is_a_fountain_filled_with_blood_dr

PART 3
EASTER
THE CRUCIFIED "KING of LOVE" is RISEN from the DEAD

Isaiah, an Old Testament prophet, is famous for his prophesies about Jesus Christ, His birth, life, death and resurrection. So, we begin in Isaiah, Chapter 53.

"Who has believed our message and to whom has the arm of the Lord been revealed? He grew up before him like a tender shoot, and like a root out of dry ground. He had no beauty or majesty to attract us to him, nothing in his appearance that we should desire him. He was despised and rejected by men, a man of sorrows, and familiar with suffering. Like one from whom men hide their faces he was despised, and we esteemed him not."

"Surely, he took up our infirmities and carried our sorrows, yet we considered him stricken by God, smitten by him, and afflicted. But he was pierced for our transgressions, he was crushed for iniquities; the punishment that brought us peace was upon him, and by his wounds we are healed. We all, like sheep, have gone astray, each of us has turned to his own way; and the Lord has laid on him the iniquity of us all."

"He was oppressed and afflicted, yet he did not open his mouth; he was led like a lamb to the slaughter, and as a sheep before her shearers is silent, so he did not open his mouth. By oppression and judgement, he was taken away. And who can speak of his descendants? For he was cut off from the land of the living; for the transgression of my people he was stricken. He was assigned a grave with the wicked, and with the rich in his death, though he has done no violence, nor was any deceit in his mouth." Isaiah 53: 1-9

Isaiah was martyred about 680 B.C. (Before the birth of Christ). So that first Christmas that Christians so love to celebrate every year was 680 years later and then our calendar began to move forward to the years named after the birth of our Lord. From year 1 – 2020 A.D. (AD stands for "Anno Domini-the Year of the Lord" or "After Divinity, meaning after Christ was born") Christians have been worshiping and celebrating the birth of Jesus Christ since 1 AD. This old, old, Story is today being recorded by this author on June 18, 2020; that is 2020 years after the birth of our Lord and Savior. In Part two, we learned about Holy Week including the death of Jesus on the Cross on Good Friday and that he was buried in a grave near the cross on Mount Calvary. Fast forward now to Sunday morning after Good Friday as recorded by Matthew, a Disciple of Jesus Christ.

"After the Sabbath, at dawn on the first day of the week. Mary Magdalene and the other Mary went to look at the tomb. There was a violent earthquake, for an angel of the Lord came down from

heaven and going to the tomb, rolled back the stone and sat on it. His appearance was like lightening, and his clothes were white as snow. The guards were so afraid of him that they shook and became like dead men."

"The angel said to the women, 'Do not be afraid, for I know that you are looking for Jesus, who was crucified. He is not here; he has risen, just as he said. Come and see the place where he lay. Then go quickly and tell the disciples: 'He has risen from the dead and is going ahead of you into Galilee. There you will see him. Now I have told you.' So, the women hurried away from the tomb, afraid yet filled with joy, and ran to tell his disciples. Suddenly Jesus met them. 'Greetings,' he said. They came to him, clasped his feet and worshiped him. Then Jesus said to them, 'Do not be afraid. Go and tell my brothers to go to Galilee; there they will see me.' While the women were on their way, some of the guards went into the city and reported to the chief priests everything that had happened. When the chief priests had met with the elders and devised a plan, they gave the soldiers a large sum of money, telling them, 'You are to say, His disciples came during the night and stole him away while we were asleep. If this report gets to the governor, we will satisfy him and keep you out of trouble.' So, the soldiers took the money and did as they were instructed. And this story has been widely circulated among the Jews to this very day." Matthew 28: 1-15

"Then the eleven disciples went to Galilee, to the mountain where Jesus had told them to go. When they saw him, they worshiped him; but some doubted. Then Jesus came to them and said, 'All authority in heaven and on earth has been given to me. Therefore, go and make disciples of all nations, baptizing them in the name of the Father and of the Son and of the Holy Spirit, and teaching them to obey everything I have commanded you. And surely, I am with you always, to the very end of the age.'" Matthew 28: 16-20

We learned earlier that some churches have a "stripping of the cross" after a Good Friday service. There is a black drape and a crown of thorns on the cross for the 40 days of Lent. Then on Easter morning worshipers each pick up a live flower (usually a carnation) and places it in the wiring that has been wrapped around the cross at the back of the sanctuary. When everyone has placed a flower and is seated, with musical background, an usher or two, depending on the size of the cross, will bring the cross forward into the Altar area. It is covered with multi-colored flowers and placed where the black draped cross had stood during Lent.

These are just a few of the different customs that this author has experienced and there are many others that you are recalling as you are reading this. One time we were given a paper and pencil and asked to write down our sins. At this Good Friday service, after the sermon, we went to the altar rail and nailed the piece of paper to the cross. Perhaps you have taken the paper outside and placed it in a bucket and then when all had participated, the paper was set on fire and the sins were burned to ashes. How about a Holy Thursday foot-washing service? The youth group took turns washing the feet of the adults in the service. These are only symbolic but can place a lasting memory in us of who Jesus is and why His Cross is central in our life. **NT – The blood of Jesus, the sinless Lamb of God, shed on the Cross of Calvary for forgiveness of sin. All people of the world can come to Jesus, confess their sin and surrender life to Him and receive the forgiveness and unconditional love of our Holy God. He is LORD!**

Christ the Lord is Risen Today

1. Christ the Lord is risen to - day,__ Al - le - lu - ia!
2. Love's re - deem - ing work is done,__ Al - le - lu - ia!
3. Lives a - gain our glo - rious King,__ Al - le - lu - ia!
4. Soar we now where Christ has led,__ Al - le - lu - ia!
*5. Hail the Lord of earth and heaven, Al - le - lu - ia!
*6. King of glo - ry, soul of bliss,__ Al - le - lu - ia!

Earth and heaven in cho - rus say,__ Al - le - lu - ia!
Fought the fight, the bat - tle won,__ Al - le - lu - ia!
Where, O death, is now thy sting?__ Al - le - lu - ia!
Fol lowing our ex - al - ted Head,__ Al - le - lu - ia!
Praise to thee by both be given,__ Al - le - lu - ia!
E - ver - las - ting life is this,__ Al - le - lu - ia!

Raise your joys and tri-umphs high, Al - le - lu - ia!
Death in vain for - bids him rise, Al - le - lu - ia!
Once he died our souls to save, Al - le - lu - ia!
Made like him, like him we rise, Al - le - lu - ia!
Thee we greet tri - um-phant now, Al - le - lu - ia!
Thee to know, thy power to prove, Al - le - lu - ia!

Text: Charles Wesley, 1739
Tune: *Lyra Davidica*, 1708

77 77D
EASTER HYMN
www.hymnary.org/text/christ_the_lord_is_risen_today_wesle
v

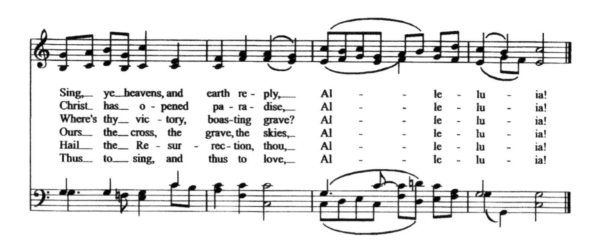

Sing,	ye heavens, and	earth re - ply,	Al	-	-	le	-	lu	-	ia!
Christ	has o - pened	pa - ra - dise,	Al	-	-	le	-	lu	-	ia!
Where's	thy vic - tory,	boas-ting grave?	Al	-	-	le	-	lu	-	ia!
Ours	the cross, the	grave, the skies,	Al	-	-	le	-	lu	-	ia!
Hail	the Re - sur -	rec - tion, thou,	Al	-	-	le	-	lu	-	ia!
Thus	to sing, and	thus to love,	Al	-	-	le	-	lu	-	ia!

THE WAY OF FAITH – Charles Wesley – 1707 -1788, wrote over 6,000 hymns after a short four month stay in the Colony of Georgia (America). www.christianity.com

On the boat from England to Georgia, the last of the colonies to be evangelized, **John and Charles Wesley** meet twenty-six German Moravians. Both brothers were impressed by the hymns singing of these evangelistic Christians and realized for the first time that hymn singing could be a spiritual experience. After his short visit, Charles, back in England, came face to face with the claims of Christ; a simple faith gripped his heart and Jesus became his Savior and Lord. His date of conversion, May 21, 1738. On that date he opened his bible and focused on one verse, **Psalm** 40:3**"He hath put a new song in my mouth; many will see and fear and will trust in the Lord."** Charles immediately organized a "Holy Club" that met every night to study the bible together and his song writing career takes off like wild fire!

The following hymns by **Charles Wesley** have "Lent to Easter" theology and are included in this devotional to enhance your worship time alone or at the family altar: **"'Tis Finished! the Messiah Dies;" "Christ the Lord is Risen Today;" "And Can it Be That I Should Gain?;"** Also, **"Hail the Day That Sees Him Rise;" "Oh, for a Thousand Tongues to Sing;"** and **"Come, Thou Long - Expected Jesus."**

And Can it Be That I Should Gain?

Text: Charles Wesley (1707-1788)
Tune: Thomas Campbell (1777-1844)

88 88 88 Refrain
SAGINA
www.hymnary.org/text/and_can_it_be_that_i_should_gain

can   it   be   That Thou,   my   God,   should   die   for   me!

How   can   it   be   That Thou, my   God,

"IT IS FINISHED"

He willingly bore the cross for me, unselfishly He set me free,

Now peace, love, joy, hope are mine, all these blessings my day intertwine;

So with thanksgiving, I move forward, denying self to serve my Lord.

Although I slip along the way, if I ask, He'll forgive, close by He'll stay.

Sometimes He nudges, sometimes He does shout, thoughts about self must be turned about.

In prayer, I listen, trusting each word; assurance in knowing His will I've heard.

Then on His way I gladly go, because towards Him I want to grow.

Wrong turns I take, failures too, but always His love sees me through.

So with prayer and praise, God's word and His song, each day I ask Jesus to walk along,

I ask Him His will be known to me; as God, the Father, made known on Calvary.

Guide me, Jesus, with my cross today, humbly, Jesus, let me repay,

You willingly bore the cross for me, unselfishly You set me free.

Shirley D. Andrews

This Jay is a large song bird known for his noisy calls. You may not be aware that this jay is known for his intelligence and complex social system with tight family bonds. Blue Jays lower their crest when they are feeding peacefully with flock members or tending to the newborn Jays. They are bossy and territorial and will chase almost anything that goes close to the nest. Both female and male are colored the same so it is difficult to tell one from the other. This is unusual in the bird world. "B-J," a name given to him for this photo, has a very attractive black band or necklace around the neck and up the side of his head. If "B-J" should get excited or aggressive his feather crest with stand up straight above his head. The oldest known wild, banded Blue Jay was at least 26 years, 11 months old. "B-J" is having some down time and is practicing mindfulness. Mindfulness may be one of the new words for meditation in 2020. However, he is very alert as well as being mindful maybe because he has become aware of a possible hawk coming a little too close. He will mimic the call of the hawk to warn his neighborhood Blue Jays to be on alert!

"You have heard that it was said, 'Love your neighbor and hate your enemies.' But I tell you; love your enemies and pray for those who persecute you, that you may be sons of your Father in heaven. He causes his sun to rise on the evil and the good, and sends rain on the righteous and the unrighteous."
Matthew 5: 43-45

It is obvious that the hawk has been an enemy of the Blue Jay and now it is necessary to notify the local Blue Jays that there is trouble up ahead. They are a close-knit flock and look out for each other. Well, that is how it is in the bird world. There could be a riff or knock out fight coming depending on the needs of the hawk. In our humanness, we have enemies that God says we are to love and not hate. This is only possible because God first loved us and he first loved our enemies. We love our enemies because God loves our enemies. God's love is perfect love and it casts out all fear. There is no fear in perfect love. We have nothing to fear by loving our enemies. Loving our enemies brings glory to God. Praying for our enemies to be blessed will release any hate we are harboring. "All things are possible with God." **Matthew 10: 27**

Prayer: Lord God, thank you for loving me and showing me why and how to love my enemies. You have forgiven me and I will forgive my enemies who may have meant to harm me. I want to obey your word and I know it will take practice and patience but I will confess and repent when I fail. Your love is everlasting love and the kind of love I want to have for all the people I meet. Help me to repay good for evil and love for hate, in Jesus' name, Amen.

Look at the amazing variety of color on this handsome fox. There is blond to reddish to dark brown fur. There are two beautiful black legs and feet with matching black trim on his whitish ears. A black nose, black whiskers and a long, dark pink tongue. It looks like spring time on the pond with melting ice and snow. This is a very cold and refreshing drink of water for a thirsty fox. Bravo, Photographer, what a prize! When this Eastern American fox is hungry, he will dine on smaller animals and also insects, fruit, berries, plants and even road kill. Perhaps this foxy father just downed a cottontail rabbit and now he runs so fast to the cold stream to satisfy his thirst. He will lap, lap, lap and then lap some more. He is a very intelligent animal and will always remember how to get to that road and then back to the same stream. He is developing a healthy pattern to sustain his family life on earth; he and his faithful mate have a very close family. The young stay around to help raise and care for the youngest ones. Males are called "dogs," females are called "vixen" and the very young are called "kits."

"I, Jesus, have sent my angel to give you this testimony for the churches. I am the Root and the Offspring of David, and the bright Morning Star. The Spirit and the bride say, 'Come!' And let him who hears say, 'Come!' Whoever is thirsty, let him come; and whoever wishes, let him take the free gift of the Water of Life.'"

Revelation 22: 16-17

These two verses come very near the end of the last book of the bible. In a way, it is Jesus giving us one more chance to choose Him over everything else in this world. Many choose Jesus through reading one or more of the four Gospels. He is either "Lord" or He is not "Lord" of our life! There is an emptiness, a thirst in every human heart that can only be satisfied by a loving and growing relationship with our Creator, Jesus, the Root and Offspring of David, the bright Morning Star. He is alive and lives in us if we have chosen to believe Him and trust Him. This verse is asking the most important question you will ever answer in this life: Do you know Jesus? Have you received the free gift of the "Water of Life?" He is the water that satisfies your thirst (inner longing). Many people know about Jesus but He wants to be personally known as your Savior and Lord. Are you thirsty for Living Water? Are you hungry for what is best and satisfies the most? This world is not our home. Our home is eternal life in heaven with Jesus.

Prayer: Lord God, Water of Life, come and fill me with love for my Heavenly Father, Jesus, my Lord and the Holy Spirit alive in me. Help me to live free with them in this "spinning out of control" world! I know I will need daily time in your presence to hear your loving voice and to satisfy my thirsty soul. Help me to nurture a life of prayer in your presence. I want and need you to guide me in the path you have for me, and thank you, God, for giving me the truth today. Now I can live in your presence and tell others about where to find "the Water of Life" who satisfies all thirst, in Jesus Christ, my Savior and Lord, Amen.

GOOD NEWS: The song of this male grosbeak sounds like an American robin in an unusually good mood. You will hear a long sing-song string of sweet whistles. Once you hear this, follow the sound until you walk up under his song perch and look for his 3 special colors. In flight, look for a distinctive pattern of big white spots in his dark wings. Besides apple blossoms, this grosbeak likes to eat sunflower and safflower seeds. Raw peanuts are also a treat that he will devour at a rapid pace. You have to admire his beauty. Red, white and black are popular colors for clothing in 2020. He is stylish in his looks and eats peanuts, people food, as well.

BAD NEWS: He builds such a flimsy nest that eggs are often visible below through the nest bottom. The male takes his turn incubating the eggs for several hours during the day and then mom takes over. She sits on the eggs the rest of the day and all night long. In the morning, when they are changing places again, they both sing quietly to each other. The male sometimes sings his normal song at full volume from inside the nest. It sounds like mom does double duty in time spent on the eggs. Dad is probably spending a lot of his time repairing the bottom of the nest. They both will be very disappointed if the eggs fall out of the bottom on to the ground. Let's not go there!

"Come, let us sing for joy to the Lord. Let us shout aloud to the rock of our salvation. Let us come before him with thanksgiving and exalt him with music and song."
Psalm 95: 1-2

God has created music as a common expression of praise for both the birds of the air and us humans who have to remain on the ground. How exciting to know that sometimes the male grosbeak shouts out his song in full volume to God. That is called exalted praise and God loves it. But the most touching part of the grosbeak praise singing is when they are changing places on the eggs and they sing to each other. What an awesome Creator God we serve and so worthy of our loudest praise. Oh, how God is glorified through these singing love birds! Let's pray with thanksgiving:

Prayer: Lord God, your Creation is so perfect. What would it be like without singing? I want to be as faithful in praise and exaltation as these precious rose-breasted grosbeaks. I am so thankful to be a small part of your plan, Lord, to fill the earth with song. Protect each flimsy grosbeak nest, Lord, so these bird families live in peace and continually send loud praises to the Throne of grace. Lord, listen to your children singing, *"I'm goin'-a* **sing** *when the Spirit says sing, (repeat two times) and obey the Spirit of the Lord. I'm goin'a* **pray** *when the Spirit says pray, (repeat two times) and obey the Spirit of the Lord. I'm goin'a* **shout** *when the Spirit says shout (repeat two times) and obey the Spirit of the Lord,* **in Jesus' name, Amen.**

(African – American Spiritual)

Meet "Olive Otter," she is resting from her labors. What has she been laboring with? Olive has been carrying her pup, baby otter, in her pouch for months and months. Her pup has been growing and growing and getting very heavy. Olive finds fish to feed her pup as he rides in her pouch and eventually, after a year or more, she releases him into the water to find his own food when he gets hungry. She is resting now but keeps a watchful eye on her pup in case she has to go and rescue him. This is a big day for her pup; he is gaining his independence but momma is very tired and hopes that they can get home safe and sound before dark. They rarely venture inland, always staying very close to water. Besides fish, otters eat sea urchins, crabs, mussels, octopus, etc. Sea otter teeth are adapted for crushing hard-shelled invertebrates such as clams and crabs. 90% of the world's Sea otters live in Alaska's coastal waters.

"You are worthy, our Lord God, to receive glory and honor and power, for you created all things, and by your will they were created and have their being."
Revelation 4: 11

If I said, now, list all the things that God has created? What is your answer after your loud groan? Oh, I know, that is impossible! And I say, you are right! But isn't it amazing to think about that? This momma otter is just one example of God's power. He spoke everything into existence with His powerful word. Every living creature our God has breathed into life and designed for living a full life on earth. We live in a fallen world with sin being our (humans) major problem. God knows when each bird or animal's life will end and He knows when our lives will end. Most important is that each day we are alive, is a day to praise our Holy God for our life; our ability to learn about sea otters; baby pups and the word of God. Let's glorify, honor and praise our Lord Jesus; for His creation; the breath of life that comes from Him every day all day long and every night all night long.

Prayer: Lord God, full of Holy power and Holy creativity, you deserve to receive glory, honor and praise today and every day for the rest of my life on earth. I am so humbled when I think about the breath of life at my birth and how you are the author of all life. You will give me my last breath before I leave earth and fall into your arms in heaven. Thank you for the faithful witness of momma sea otter; she is beautiful and fills my heart with your love. Forgive me, Lord, when I take so little time to give you the glory, honor and praise that you are so worthy of. I am often rebellious about taking enough time daily to show you my gratitude for your beautiful life intertwined with mine. Without you, I am nothing and can do nothing. I love you with my highest praise and I take this time to remind the world that you have given precious life to all living things, all glory to you, my Holy God, who continually breathes life into His creation all day and all night, in Jesus' name, Amen.

WOOD DUCK – *dressed to impress*

Aix sponsa

Duanesburg, New York

Fairly common

Not only is "Wonderful Woody" the best dressed duck in town, he also is well known for being the only duck in North America that regularly produces two broods in one year. And, if that is not enough recognition, he is the most stunningly colorful of all waterfowl. Look for wood ducks in and around ponds. Woody likes to hang out around the edges of swamps, sluggish streams, overgrown beaver ponds and woody marshes. Wood ducks mate in pairs in January and most birds arriving at the breeding ground are already paired. Can you imagine arriving at the scene when courtship begins? The wood duck shows off his colorful plumage with a special dance with spectacular choreography that attracts the nearest female. This guy, Wonderful Woody, found his mate in winter and now they arrive together at their nesting place and when spring arrives one of the two broods will be born. After hatching, the ducklings will jump as far as fifty feet to the ground and slowly make their way to the water. The oldest recorded wood duck was a male at least twenty-two and a half years old. He was banded in Oregon and found in California. God loves and protects His wood ducks, no doubt about it! But God's love for you is so much greater because He made you in His image! Praise His name!

"When Joseph's brothers saw that their father was dead, they said, 'what if Joseph holds a grudge against us and pays us back for all the wrongs, we did to him?' So, they sent word to Joseph, saying, 'your father left instruction before he died: This is what you are to say to Joseph: I ask you to forgive your brothers the sins and the wrongs they committed in treating you so badly. Now please forgive the sins of the servants of the God of your father.' When their message came to him, Joseph wept. His brothers then came and threw themselves down before him. 'We are your slaves,' they said."
Genesis 50:15-18

Joseph's father gives him a beautiful coat of many colors, much like Woody's, but does not give his other sons anything so beautiful to wear. This story about Joseph, his father's favorite son, brings burning jealousy to the hearts of the sons who feel unloved by their father and they want to do much harm to Joseph. But the verses above show reconciliation and forgiveness to all and the story does have a gloriously happy ending and a wonderful lesson for all those reading this page. Do you think Woody's duck friends are jealous of his gorgeous coat of many colors? How would you feel if you were one of Joseph's brothers? Can you forgive your father? Let's pray about it:

Prayer: Lord God, Healer of hurts and wounds that have been stirred up. You have made a way through Jesus, who bled and died on the Cross for my sins. You ask me to forgive others so they are set free from the burden of sin and can live a peaceful life in the power of the Holy Spirit, the gift that you gave on the first Pentecost. Help me today, Lord, to live a life that glorifies you and forgives others who need to know and love you, in Jesus' name, Amen.

The English name, Turkey, may have originated from the country of Turkey as early shipping routes passed through that country on the way to English markets. In the 1940's people began catching these wild birds and transported them to many other areas. Such transplants allowed wild turkeys to spread to all lower 48 states plus Hawaii and parts of southern Canada. Male wild turkeys provide no parental care for mom or the chicks, unlike so many other bird species. Newly hatched chicks follow their mother. She feeds them for a few days until they learn to find food on their own. As the chicks grow, they band into groups composed of several hens (females) and their broods (many chicks). It sounds like a church community that not only worships together but also studies the bible together, prays together and serves the community together. In the winter the wild turkeys, who band together, can exceed 200 turkeys. They obviously all get along well and benefit from being gregarious, patient and loving. Another area of interest: while taking a turkey home is considered a brag-worthy feat, being called one is considered an insult. Historical accounts suggest the phrase came about from the day to day bartering between Colonists and Indians over wild turkeys.

"Love is patient, love is kind. It does not envy, it does not boast, it is not proud. It is not rude, it is not self-seeking, it is not easily angered and keeps no record of wrongs. Love does not delight in evil but rejoices with the truth. It always protects, always trusts, always hopes and always perseveres."
1 Corinthians 13: 4-7

On Mother's Day let's remember to give God praise not only for our own moms but what about those hard-working turkey moms? They are blessed by God because instinctively they enjoy being together in large groups and taking care of the young is a priority. They can all help each other at meal time and when a chick gets lost or a chick gets an illness. They can sing together and make a lot of loud praise music. They live sharing God's love even though they cannot know God personally as we can. God gave us a heart like His so we can love God, love others and love ourselves. God loves His turkeys and He protects them from extinction. We can love God because He first loved us. He sacrificed His own life for us on the Cross. I hope you have a Cross in your church where all can see it. Let's pray now to love God and each other just like God says in 1Corintians 13.

Prayer: Lord God, thank you for your faithful love. Help me to be a patient lover, kind to all with no envy in me. Keep me from boasting or being prideful. Help me put the needs of others before my own needs. Correct me when I get it wrong. Teach me the truth about love so I can love others like you love them. I love you, Lord, for being so patient with me and for paying in full for my sins on the heavy Cross you carried up that steep hill on the first Good Friday. You are the indescribable gift sent from heaven to save all, in Jesus' name, Amen.

Precious Readers, receive "the beauty and warmth of God's love" as you enjoy this photo. God's Son, Jesus Christ, has so much love, forgiveness, grace, goodness, peace and joy to anoint you with. It is the gift of the Holy Spirit that He gives to us for our freedom, enjoyment, purpose and protection. He changes lives forever and He promises you will never be the same; your heart will be filled with God's light, His forgiving love, His peace, joy and hope. This is the message of the Cross of Calvary. Jesus, our sinless Savior, paid your sin debt! Today is July 23, 2020 and we are social distancing, wearing protective masks and enduring lockdowns as a result of the worldwide coronavirus pandemic of 2019-20 which started in China. God is always in control and we can no longer ignore the obvious! America repent; God is waiting with open arms to get us back to worshiping Him in Spirit and in Truth; to law and order, instead of anarchy; to living with godly purpose; with a peaceful existence through a relationship with Him, Jesus Christ. Can we give up busyness; doing our own self-centered agendas? When Mary and Joseph, after three days, couldn't find their 12- year- old, they finally found him in the Temple. **Jesus said "didn't you know I had to be in my Father's house?" Luke 2:49.** Can we join Him with this same common purpose of building His kingdom? God is to be praised for His extraordinary creation and His plan for His peace in all storms. Our Lord will never leave us or forsake us; but there will be more storms. This Covid-19 storm will end but **God's love never ends!** God's one requirement is faith in Him and what He did on the Cross of Calvary. "**Faith the size of a mustard seed will move mountains." Matthew 17: 20.**

"So that Christ may dwell in your hearts through faith. And I pray that you, being rooted and established in love, may have power together with all the Lord's holy people, to grasp how wide and long and high and deep is the love of Christ, and to know this love that surpasses knowledge – that you may be filled to the measure of all the fullness of God."
Ephesians 3: 17-19

We pray in faith believing, God moves. We pray again and again; God moves more and more. We worship from the heart and God is glorified. This is the joyful, peaceful work of all "born again" Christians. Keep God at the center of everything in your life. He is LORD!

Prayer: Lord God, Loving Savior, my Prince of Peace all through the storms of life, forgive my self-centeredness. My life of busyness could lead to ignoring or forgetting who is in charge. Lord, help me daily to focus on you; enjoying your presence and receiving your love. Help me to tell the world that my "God so loved the world that He gave His one and only Son that whosoever believes in Him shall not perish but have eternal life." Now, Abba Father, daddy so very dear, bless all our readers with the peace that passes all understanding. Bless their lives and families with the wide, long, high and deep love of Christ, the love that surpasses knowledge, so to be filled to the measure of all the fullness of God, in the glorious name of Jesus Christ and Him crucified, Amen.

Hail the Day That Sees Him Rise

1 Hail the day that sees him rise, Alleluia! to his throne beyond the skies. Alleluia! Christ, the Lamb for sinners given, Alleluia! enters now the highest heaven. Alleluia!

2 There for him high triumph waits; Alleluia! lift your heads, eternal gates. Alleluia! He has conquered death and sin; Alleluia! take the King of glory in. Alleluia!

3 Highest heaven its Lord receives; Alleluia! yet he loves the earth he leaves. Alleluia! Though returning to his throne, Alleluia! still he calls us all his own. Alleluia!

4 Still for us he intercedes; Alleluia! his atoning death he pleads, Alleluia! near himself prepares our place, Alleluia! he the first-fruits of our race. Alleluia!

5 There we shall with you remain, Alleluia! partners of your endless reign, Alleluia! see you with unclouded view, Alleluia! find our heaven of heavens in you. Alleluia!

Text: Charles Wesley, 1739, and Thomas
  Cotterill, 1820, alt.
Tune: Robert Williams, 1817

77 77 with alleluias
LLANFAIR
www.hymnary.org/text/hail_the_day_that_sees_him_rise

Oh, for a Thousand Tongues to Sing

6 Hear him, you deaf; you voiceless ones,
your loosened tongues employ;
you blind, behold your Savior come;
and leap, you lame, for joy!

7 To God all glory, praise, and love
be now and ever given
by saints below and saints above,
the church in earth and heaven.

Text: Charles Wesley, 1739, alt.
Tune: Carl G. Gläser, 1828, adapt. and arr.
Lowell Mason, 1839

CM
AZMON
www.hymnary.org/text/o_for_a_thousand_tongues_to_sing_my

Come, Thou Long-Expected Jesus

Text: Charles Wesley, 1744
Tune: Rowland H. Prichard, 1830;
  harm. from *The English Hymnal*, 1906

87 87D
HYFRYDOL
www.hymnary.org/text/come_thou_long_expected_jesus_born_to

WERE YOU THERE?

Were you there when they crucified my Lord?
Were you there when they crucified my Lord?
Oh! sometimes it causes me to tremble, tremble, tremble.
Were you there when they crucified my Lord?

Were you there when they nailed him to the tree?
Were you there when they nailed him to the tree?
Oh! sometimes it causes me to tremble, tremble, tremble.
Were you there when they nailed him to the tree?

Were you there when they pierced him in the side?
Were you there when they pierced him in the side?
Oh! sometimes it causes me to tremble, tremble, tremble.
Were you there when they pierced him in the side?

Were you there when the sun refused to shine?
Were you there when the sun refused to shine?
Oh! sometimes it causes me to tremble, tremble, tremble.
Were you there when the sun refused to shine?

Were you there when they laid him in the tomb?
Were you there when they laid him in the tomb?
Oh! sometimes it causes me to tremble, tremble, tremble.
Were you there when they laid him in the tomb?
African-American Spiritual

PHOTOGRAPHER
J. Michael Fuller

Mike holds bachelor and master's degrees from Albany State University in Albany, NY. He spent 28 years as a 5th and 6th grade teacher, specializing in science. Many students in the Scotia-Glenville School District in Scotia, NY benefitted from Mike's expertise in teaching about the world around us, above us and beyond. He passed on to his students a love for learning, a respect for each other and a respect for God's creation. Mike and his wife also taught Sunday school for many years before she passed away several years ago.

In retirement, Mike continues his life-long passion for photography. He has been published on "Ranger Rick" and "Audubon" covers, Sierra Club and Audubon Society calendars, and published in "International Wildlife" and other publications. He travels extensively in pursuit of new close up shots of God's magnificent creatures. He lives in Duanesburg, NY on his 42 acres with ponds, woods and hills to climb. His woods are full of songbirds, maybe because he has delicious bird feeders scattered strategically around his quiet property.

Mike continues to use his photography ministry to bless others, including those who read "DIVINE LOVE" – Lent – Holy Week- Easter, a Devotional Inspired by Nature: Volume 4. He also volunteers in Youth Ministry when not on the road or in an airplane with his camera.

AUTHOR
Shirley D. Andrews

Shirley is a graduate of the Eastman School of Music in Rochester, NY and has a master's degree from the Crane School of Music in Potsdam, NY. She taught elementary public-school music for 31 years. Most of those years were in Scotia-Glenville School District. She also taught music education classes at Schenectady County Community College. She loved her career in teaching and Music ministry. She has two children and two grandchildren.

After retirement and the death of her husband, Shirley pursued a career as a Certified Lay Minister in the Upper New York Annual Conference, Adirondack District of the United Methodist Church. She has held leadership positions at Porter Corners UMC, Ballston Spa UMC, and led worship at Woodlawn Commons in the Wesley Community. Having recently moved to a new community, she is now a member of the Amsterdam United Methodist Church in Amsterdam, NY. She continues to be passionate about devotional writing for God lovers, God seekers, nature lovers and the family altar. A future project might be "FAITH FOR AN UPSIDE-DOWN WORLD" – Resurrection to Pentecost: A Devotional Inspired by Nature: Volume 5.

REFERENCES

Book of North American Birds, The Reader's Digest Association, Inc. Pleasantville, NY/Montreal – 1990

Peterson Field Guide to Birds of Eastern and Central North America by Roger Tory Peterson; text copyright 2010 by the Marital Trust B – sixth edition

National Audubon Society Field guide to North American Birds – Eastern Region; copyright 1994 by Chanticleer Press, Inc. – second edition

www.nationalgeographic.com

Oxford Dictionary, published, created and produced in the United States and Great Britain in 1998 by Dorling Kindersley Limited and Oxford University Press, Inc.

Good Friday Message by Rev. Judy Humphrey-Fox – 2020, printed with permission from the Author.

www.wikipedia.com – North American wildlife in wilderness areas.

Holy Bible – NIV – Copyright 1990 – Zondervan Publishing House, Grand Rapids, Michigan – second edition.

Zondervan Exhaustive Concordance – NIV – 1999, Zondervan Publishing House, Grand Rapids, Michigan – second edition

www.audubon.org

www.allaboutbirds.com

www.birds.cornell.edu

www.alaskawildlife.org

www.hymnary.com

www.biblegateway.com

AVAILABLE NOW
Author – Shirley D. Andrews
Photographer – J. Michael Fuller
www.shirleydandrews.com

"His Eye is on the Sparrow," a Devotional Inspired by Nature: Volume 1

"His Eye is on the Sparrow," a Devotional Inspired by Nature: Volume 2

"MERRY CHRISTMAS: Advent to Epiphany," a Devotional Inspired by Nature: Volume 3

"DIVINE LOVE: Lent – Holy Week – Easter," a Devotional Inspired by Nature: Volume 4

COMING SOON
"FAITH for an Upside-Down World: Resurrection to Pentecost," a Devotional Inspired by Nature:
Volume 5

"Though He Died Young, Yet He Speaks"
By
Shirley D. Andrews

A memoir of generations of faith, love and prayer has its beginning in the 1700's with the Rev. Zadok Hunn. He graduates from Yale College in 1766 when Yale was new and known as a seminary for men with Christian roots in England. He rides horseback on dusty, rutty and sometimes muddy trails, rain or shine, preaching the Gospel of Jesus Christ. The young pastor, filled with the Holy Spirit, gallops from small hamlet to small hamlet, tirelessly spreading the "Good News." Though he died young, his achievements were tremendous, and now several generations later he is still speaking.

This is an historical memoir of a pioneer family that still walks by faith and cherishes their Christian upbringing. All five of us, daughters and sons of Elmer and Ruth DeSmith, are excited about meeting face to face with Jesus first in heaven; then we want to meet Zadok Hunn to say "thank you for being an enormous encourager to all of our family who found a personal relationship with Jesus Christ during our lifetime on earth." Zadok, your prayers and the prayers of those you evangelized were faithfully answered by our loving, gracious and merciful God." We, the children of Elmer and Ruth DeSmith, are now elderly, 70's and 80's but the Good News is: We are excited about seeing Jesus in heaven and will thank you, Zadok, in person, for praying us into God's Kingdom. **We Now Know That:**

THE BEST IS YET TO COME!

Printed in the United States
by Baker & Taylor Publisher Services